ALL ABOUT REIKI

Your Beginner's Guide to Discovering What Reiki Is, Healing and Self Treatments, Attunements, Your Seven Chakras, Performing Aura Viewings, and the Reiki Symbols

TIMOTHY GEHRANG

All About Reiki: What is Reiki, How to Do Reiki Healing, How an Attunement is Performed, the Seven Chakras, Aura Viewings, Reiki Symbols and Their Uses, and Self Treatments with Reiki
Timothy Gehrang

Copyright © 2011 by Timothy Gehrang

Published solely by Timothy Gehrang

The ideas, procedures, and suggestions contained in this book are not intended as a substitute for consulting with your physician. All matters regarding your health require medical supervision. The author shall not be liable or responsible for any loss or damage allegedly arising from any information or suggestion in this book.

This book or parts thereof may not be reproduced in any form, stored in a retrieval system, or transmitted in any form by any means - electronic, mechanical, photocopy, recording, or otherwise - without prior written permission of the publisher, author or legal representative of both parties, except as provided by United States of America copyright law.

All rights reserved.

Foreword

This book opens a window for you to the wonderful world of Reiki. A window that gives you short insights of what Reiki is and of what Reiki can do for you. You'll see, it is very easily readable.

We have provided the book with lots of real-life examples of how Reiki works. We have also provided it with numerous exercises; they will prove to you that Reiki is a reality. Not any reality, but the one that was always inside you, without you knowing it. Discover the truth within. You'll discover the one and only Truth.

Table of Contents

Chapter I – Reiki: The Secret Art of Happiness, the Miraculous Medicine ---------------- 1
    What is Reiki? -------------------- 1
    How Does Reiki Work? ------------- 2
    How Does Reiki Heal? ------------- 3
    Does Reiki Really Work? ---------- 5
    Has There Really Been Any Clinical Evidence That Reiki Works? --------- 5
    Are There Any Side Effects of Reiki? -- 6
    Is Reiki Comparable to Other Energy Practices? ---------------------- 7
    What About People Who Don't Believe in Reiki? -------------------------- 8
    Are There Some Tips for Activating Your Reiki? ------------------------ 9
    Is it Possible to Practice Reiki on Yourself? ----------------------- 10
    Can the Reiki be Lost? ------------- 10
    The Happy State of Flow ----------- 11
    The Other Benefits of Reiki --------- 12
Chapter II: Chakras and Aura ----------- 13
    What are Chakras? ----------------- 13
    Before for Exercising Chakras -------- 14
    How We Describe the Various Chakras 17

Base/Root Chakra ... 18
Sacral Chakra ... 19
Solar Plexus Chakra ... 21
Heart Chakra ... 22
Throat Chakra ... 24
Eyebrow Chakra (The Third Eye) ... 25
Crown Chakra ... 26
How You Can Check Your Chakras ... 28
Aura – The Subtle Sign of Your (Im)Perfection ... 29
5 Steps to Seeing Auras ... 30
Chapter III – Initiation in Reiki ... 33
Can Everyone Become a Reiki Practitioner or a Reiki Master? ... 33
What Must You Do to Become a Reiki Practitioner? ... 34
How Much Would an Attunement Cost? ... 37
Can I Self-Attune Myself to Reiki? ... 37
Can Reiki Attunements be Done Online? ... 38
Can Reiki Attunements be Done in Groups? ... 39
What You Will Learn at Reiki Level 1, 2 and 3 ... 41
What, in Fact, are Reiki Symbols? ... 45

The Reiki Symbols Explained 46
Cho Ku Rei (CKR) 47
Sei He Ki (SHK) 49
Hon Sha Ze Sho Nen (HSZSN) 51
Dai Ko Mio (DKM) 53
How is a Reiki Attunement Performed? 54
Is it Possible to Learn Reiki in 4 to 5 Days? 54
Visualizing Symbol Energy 55
How to Visualize Symbol Energy 55

Chapter IV – Reiki Uses and Techniques .. 56
Hand Positions in Reiki Healing 56
Self Treatment Hand Positions 56
Quick Self-Treatment 58
Healing Others 59
Replacing Negative Energy, Step-by-Step 59
Reiki Healing Benefits 61
Using Reiki Together with Other Healing Methods 64

Chapter V – Reiki Use for Wealth 66
Reiki and Karma 66
Reiki Projects for Wealth 67
How to Write a Project to Reach Your Goals 68

Chapter I – Reiki: The Secret Art of Happiness, the Miraculous Medicine

What is Reiki?

There is an aura of mystery surrounding this "secret art of inviting happiness," "miraculous medicine for all diseases" (Reiki prayer). In fact, the mystery only comes from the fact that very few people are Reiki initiated – and the rest just have heard about Reiki as an "Oriental exotic something about uncertain mystic energy."

Reiki's etymology is simple, as the phrase is formed of two Japanese words: Rei (soul, spirit) and Ki (vital energy). As a free translation then, Reiki would mean "the energy that comes from the Spirit (the One)," the "universal force." Of course, numerous definitions have been given to Reiki. What is to be remembered is that a Reiki practitioner passes this energy (ki, chi, prana, light, holy ghost, whatever you would wish to call it) directly to the patient's body, plugging her/ him directly to the Universal Energy.

The secret is long time not a secret, as it has been known to Eastern civilizations for millennia. In fact, the far Orient is the cradle of what we call now "traditional healing methods," in opposition to "medical methods."

When saying Reiki, almost nobody thinks of its universal energy meaning; the noun Reiki has become synonym to "healing technique," more precisely "hand healing technique."

Reiki was developed by a Japanese Shinto monk, Mikao Usui, during early 1920s. The legend says he has received the Reiki symbols by a divine revelation, while having a 21 day retreat on a sacred mountain near his town. When back home, he founded a school where he wanted to teach the path to enlightenment. In its early days, Reiki was an initiation process and it took the students several years to become Masters. Once brought to the western world, Usui Shiki Reiki Ryoho was essentially simplified and turned into a healing technique. Over the years, several schools detached from Usui Reiki – Dolphin Reiki, Quantum Reiki, Mayan Reiki and so on.

One thing to have in mind: you can't avoid Reiki, for any reason, if you want to get something out of your present existence. Reiki is the shortest path to… many things. You will discover them inside this book.

How Does Reiki Work?

Overlapping the physical body at the most minute detail, we are given – at birth – an energetic body. Through the spine channel, chakras and meridians, the Universal Energy (Reiki) is fed to every cell of the physical body. Reiki is the element that makes us live – for without Reiki, we are only decaying flesh. Reiki is the blueprint of any being.

The principles and elements used with Reiki (Universal energy, energy plexuses, energy channels, energy mastery, energy healing, etc.) are common to the majority of initiatory schools in different civilizations (Egyptian, Hebrew, Greek, Mayan, Hindu, Chinese).

In a healthy body, the Reiki is flowing naturally and makes the organism function normally. Whenever a block obstructs the spine, a chakra or a meridian, an energetic imbalance happens. We shall further on see that each chakra is responsible for a series of internal organs. If not removed on time, the imbalance will turn into a dis-ease and then into an illness (installed at the organ governed by the corresponding blocked chakra).

How Does Reiki Heal?

For a better understanding of the phenomenon, let us compare the body to a television set, and Reiki to the television program you receive. The radio signal is crystal clear – your neighbor watches the same show – but your TV set in not functioning well. One if its components (chakras) is not working as it should, and at some point in the future, the TV unit will crash.

You have two "healing" possibilities for your TV set defective part: either have it repaired when still working (Reiki), or throw it away when permanently damaged (surgery).

The Reiki practitioner would feel the imbalance with his palms, or even see it with his third eye. He would not give you a diagnostic; he would simply detect an imbalance in your energetic field. He would ask for the Reiki to come and heal you. As a principle, the universal energy will then channel through his hands and repair your imbalance, all by itself, without any need to be precisely targeted, directed, pushed or pulled. The Reiki will automatically fill in the gaps, clean the negative energy, then smooth its flow inside your organism. That is because the Reiki knows **what** and **how** to heal.

In fact, for advanced practitioners, there is no need of the hands: they can send the Reiki by looking at you, by looking at your picture or by thinking of you, in your absence.

This is due to Reiki being about intention; the intention to call for the Reiki over the patient and the intention of the patient to receive the Reiki.

Does Reiki Really Work?

Reiki works in almost any physical, emotional, or mental problems. It helps fractures to heal a lot faster, it relieves pain, it detoxifies the organism, it can even help alleviate cancer symptoms. It can do **so many** things you wouldn't ever imagine!

There are two factors to take into consideration when talking about Reiki's healing power:
1. The therapist. The more advanced and experienced he is, the better his or her results. This is because, with time and with practice, s/he would enhance his channeling capacity, and would also know better **what** to do and **how** to perform Reiki. Very advanced practitioners might send the healing energy just with the power of a smile or of a benevolent attitude.
2. The patient. S/he doesn't only have to **allow** the Reiki, but s/he also has to **accept** to let it work.

Has There Really Been Any Clinical Evidence That Reiki Works?

After a certain age, men generally suffer from back pains, without any clinical sign of injury; it just hurts. After being attuned and beginning the self-therapy period, most men will remember, at a certain moment, that they **had** a chronic back pain. All Reiki beginners have reported amelioration of their general or particular states; they sleep better, they don't catch cold, migraines cease, articulation pains ease, etc. And all these only took them the three weeks between the first and the second level attunements!

The most common electronic medical tests – EEG and EKG – show better brain and heart performance with people who have been attuned.

Are There Any Side Effects of Reiki?

A common joke of the therapists states that "Reiki is like an aspirin: if it doesn't do good, at least it won't hurt."

Strange as it might be – as a definition, Reiki would be "the white intelligent energy coming from the Supreme Being" – there should be no side effects at all.

Reiki is an intelligent force – it knows what to do to balance every organ, but you need to address it to **that** specific organ. That being said, no side effects should occur other than a feeling of relaxation.

Is Reiki Comparable to Other Energy Practices?

No matter if it is Yoga, or Qui Gong, or Tai Chi, or Kung Fu, or Acupuncture, or bio-energy healing, they all operate with the same Universal energy transmitted through the same channels to the same chakras and to the same organs (or to the exterior), and the benefits are almost the same. They just name it differently. Let us see what is uniting and what is differentiating these practices:

a) Yoga regulates Reiki flow. Yogis call it Prana. Unlike Reiki, Yoga is also a workout for the physical body. The final aims are health and enlightenment.
b) Qui Gong regulates Reiki flow. Practitioners call it Qui. Unlike Reiki, Qui Gong is also a workout for the physical body. The final aims are health and enlightenment.
c) Tai Chi is very similar to Qui Gong. The final aim is enlightenment.
d) Kung Fu is very similar to Qui Gong and Tai Chi. The intermediate aim is mastering the martial art, but the final aims are health and enlightenment.
e) Acupuncture heals the body by regulating Reiki flow. The final aim is health.
f) Bio-energy healing does the job very

similarly to Reiki, but the energy comes from the healer, not from the Universal Power. Bio-energy therapists might get very tired after a healing session, when their personal energy has to fill in a deep rupture in the patient's energy field.

g) Reiki regulates Reiki flow. Unlike parts a) to f) above, Reiki is not only addressing one self's health, but it was conceived as a tool to heal others, too, while the healer is still searching for the final self-realization.

Reiki is extremely easy to learn and to apply. In fact, it is the shortest and the easiest spiritual path.

What About People Who Don't Believe in Reiki?

Fear and mistrust are only the result of not knowing. Here is a very short, funny and useful exercise you can do all by yourself and see if there is any result at all. You should know that, because every person on the face of this planet has the subtle energetic system embedded since birth, everyone can master the Reiki.

Sit or stand in a quiet room, where nobody could disturb the process. Sit rather, as the exercise should last for ten minutes. Put your hands on your knees, palms facing each other at the same height. In a very slow motion, approach your hands in a symmetrical movement. Focus your attention on your palms and fingers. Do the movement several times with your eyes open, then shut them and continue. Don't haste, take your time – you might have a revelation.

At a certain moment, depending on your sensitivity, you will feel the hands tingle, as if a very weak electrical current were passing between. Continue until the sensation is permanent. When the tingling is steady, stop your hands a few inches apart. Bend the fingers (don't touch them, though), as if you were holding a five-inch ball. Begin to move the hands in a slow manner, as if you were comforting the imaginary ball. Within a few minutes, you will certainly feel the materiality of the ball. The tingling will intensify and your hands could also become warmer, or even hot.

Are There Some Tips for Activating Your Reiki?

The exercise above is the first step towards meeting the Reiki. We have also offered you specific exercises in the Chakra chapter. You will see there that the Reiki is, in fact, already working in your body.

Is it Possible to Practice Reiki on Yourself?

Definitely, yes. The self-treatment after being attuned is nothing else than practicing Reiki on yourself.

You will experience brand new, empowering, soothing, beautiful sensations. A sudden understanding of past and present events will emerge from your deepest subconscious. You will undergo a complete shift in awareness.

Sometimes, after being attuned in the third level, you will be permanently connected with both Father God and Mother Earth in the same time. You won't be able to wipe a subtle fine smile out of your face, because you are permanently happy.

It is the moment when you will understand every little thing that happens to you: why they happen and what they teach you.

Can the Reiki be Lost?

Never. We have already told you that Reiki is the energy that gives you life – which means **it is** there since before birth, since conception.

Any Reiki practitioner has had periods when s/he couldn't be able to practice for a few days. Or even has forgotten about practicing for a longer period.

The only thing that could happen is a

process of slowing the Reiki down, of braking it, as if mud had been deposited on the sides of your energetic piping.

The problem can be solved in a matter of days.

But, if you had already reached the state of flow, of permanent connection to the Reiki, you can't leave it: it is so pleasant and beneficial that your being will never be able to let it go.

The Happy State of Flow

Continuous practice of self-treatment and meditation connects you more and more to the Reiki, until it will become a permanent sensation. You will be able to sense your chakras and the spine filled with energy at any given moment. Moreover, if you decide to concentrate upon them for a few seconds, the sensation of them being fully vivid and operational will be almost physically strong.

If your energetic system was already balanced before the attunements, you can feel the state of flow after the first level attunement. If less sensitive, after receiving the Master attunement, you will certainly remain in touch with the Reiki.

What is the state of flow? Nothing other than being connected to the Power. It showers upon you like a fine light rain, and it flows within you like an electric current. You literally feel it. The sensation is going on when eating, working, walking in the street, always.

The Other Benefits of Reiki

There are lots of benefits to Reiki, beside the already listed ones.

One huge effect of Reiki is your connection to All That Is. Don't think it is a being. No, you are connected to everything that was, is, and will be. Reiki integrates the practitioner into the **permanence** dimension. Plus, your mind will know no space: here or there, your home or the "center" of the Universe are in the **same place**.

Your will is the will of the entire Universe. Reiki, your Guardian Angel, Beings of Light will work together with you for the fulfillment of your wishes.

Chapter II: Chakras and Aura

What are Chakras?

Before going any further, we need to understand what chakras are, the way they function and their influence over our bodies. Chakras are of utmost importance, no matter what the "occult" training is you want to participate in. Yoga, Martial Arts, Thai Chi etc. they all deal with subtle energies and frequencies.

The exercises below are designed for people who only want to have a vague sensation of what a Reiki session is. This would be fitting for people who don't trust Reiki, but are curious about it. Before deciding if they want to have an attunement – or not – the exercises allow a sensitivity raise in the palms and in the chakras. The sensations might be noticeable for most people, but could be strong for those who are either already sensitive or have gone through meditation trainings. For some people, the awakening of the energy self-awareness could even be dramatic, with revelation values.

The energy difference between an average, healthy, well balanced chakra human on the street and a 3rd degree Reiki practitioner is like 100:1,600; every degree doubles your energy field: 100% before the attunement, 200% after the first degree, 400% after the second, 800% after the third, 1,600% as a Master beginner. The two-fold goes on with practice…

Before Exercising Chakras

1. You can do an exercise per chakra per day and repeat it three times a day. In seven days you will have an idea about subtle energies.
2. Don't over-exercise over one single chakra (like ten times a day and/or seven days in a row).
3. The purpose of the exercises is just to let you know about Reiki. For further knowledge, please do have your attunements done by your personal Reiki Master.
4. Do the exercises slowly, paying attention not only to the movements, but also to the sensations going through your mind and body.
5. The largest part of Reiki is intention. Do intend to feel every part of your body where the energy goes, do intend to raise your energy, and it will happen.
6. Your breathing does not matter at this level. Breathe naturally. Have the windows open, for you need as much

oxygen as possible.
7. If you are a sensitive person, then you might suffer from a sort of "electric shock" in the chakra you are rehearsing. Stop. Don't repeat – you could harm yourself badly.

Chakra derives from Sanskrit and means "wheel." The initiated, or the ordinary people who have the "third eye" open, say they look like "wheels of luminous energy." Chakras are energetic centers situated along the main energetic meridian of the body – the spine. They correspond to the nervous plexuses of the physical body. Hence, today's generic meaning of the noun chakra: energetic center. Chakras relate to endocrine glands situated **inside** the body, and that is why they have two projections on the exterior: front and back, at approximately the same height of the spine.

Plexuses are like intersections in the nervous system: the spinal cord highway branches into roads that branch into streets and then alleys, going from the brain to the organs, and to the cells. Chakras and energetic meridians overlap the nervous system and its ganglions, conducting the Universal Life Force to the cells, giving life to the organism.

But chakras do not perform this function only; they are also energy antennae of our being. We receive same-frequency vibrations from the universe, and we emit vibration into the universe, 360° around, on a sphere model. This is the way we connect with everything, this is the way we feel the auras of the others, and have sympathies or antipathies. This is the way we meet "coincidences," this is the way we have telepathies.

Each chakra is governing one subtle body. When the main channel (along the backbone) is clean and allowing the Universal energy to flow, and when chakras are well-balanced, the subtle bodies extend more and more in the exterior. This chakra function is the one that lets others feel your presence "at a first glance;" in fact, their aura comes in contact with yours – they will unconsciously feel your energetic personality.

A blocked or a low energy chakra affects our functioning. Health, emotions, mind, behavior, wealth, relationships, vitality – everything might fall apart if the energy level is not set again to an optimum value.

Chakras are said to have different colors, but people who have meditated for long time say there is no color attached to them, and that the color-motif is just a technique for deeper concentration. Despite this opinion, auras **do show** an array of colors corresponding to the colors of the chakras.

How We Describe the Various Chakras

Before listing the main characteristics of the chakras, let us describe the notions we have used:

Position: the exact place on the physical body where the chakra is situated.

Element: the Japanese Shinto system relates chakras to the main six elements that form our "reality": earth, water, air, fire, ether, thought.

Sentence: each of the chakra is responsible for one level of our existence; "I have," the sentence for the root chakra, is the lowest level – that of our material needs, while "I know," the sentence for the crown chakra, means "I am one with the One, then I know everything."

Color: each chakra is said to have a color, correspondent to the colors of the light spectrum.

Subtle body: each chakra is the origin and the transmitter of an aura; the ethereal body (root chakra) corresponds to the earthly, material existence, while the karmic body (crown chakra) corresponds to the unification with the One, and to the moment the karma is "burnt out."

Body: every chakra sends Reiki to all organs near it.

Issues: problems occurring when the chakra is imbalanced (under-activated).

When activated: the normal health and mind state of a human being; we have also given examples of over-activation).

Inserting means gently pushing the energy ball into your body.

Base/Root Chakra

Position: perineum area (between scrotum and anus – for men – and vagina and anus – for women)
Element: earth
Sentence: I have
Color: red
Subtle body: ethereal
Body: spine, kidneys, legs, feet, rectum, immune system
Issues: fear, lack of motivation, insecurity, uncertainty, lack of vital energy
When activated: strength, power, eagerness for well-being and for wealth, energy, attractiveness. When over-activated: selfishness, cruelty, violence, greed.
Exercise: stand up, feet shoulders wide. Point your palms towards the ground, then turn them slowly upwards, as if digging the earthly energy beneath your soles. Don't bend, do it with the fingers, then with the palms, bending the elbows. Pull the energy slowly up along your feet, legs, knees, thighs. Insert it into the root chakra. Do the movement seven times. Feel the tingling in your palms when you grasp the energy, feel the tingling when inserting it into the base chakra. Spend a few minutes with your attention focused

into the "root" area, palms resting against it. Do not cross hands, do not cross fingers, keep fingers together. Repeat the exercise two or three times per day.

General information: The root chakra links us to Mother Earth and her energy. It is called "root" because the Universal energy, flowing down the spine, leaves this chakra through the feet and ramifies inside the earth like a root. Through the same "root," Mother Earth send us vitality, the power of existing and **having** everything we need.

Sacral Chakra

Position: two inches below the navel, one inch inside (push with your fingertip – the place where it hurts is the center of the chakra)
Element: water
Sentence: I want, I feel
Color: orange
Subtle body: emotional
Organs: sexual organs, bladder, kidney, adrenal glands, lower intestines
Issues: if too active - lust for money and power, lack of self-control, low morality; if blocked - low libido, lack of wish to live, lack of sexyness, urinary problems
When activated: capacity on enjoying living, attractiveness, increased libido, positive

emotions, and pleasure

Exercise: stand up, feet shoulders wide. Point your palms towards the ground, then turn them slowly upwards, as if digging the earthly energy beneath your soles. Don't bend, do it with the fingers, then with the palms, bending the elbows. Pull the energy slowly up along your feet, legs, knees, thighs, root chakra. Insert it into the sacral chakra. Do the movement seven times. Feel the tingling in your palms when you grasp the energy, feel the tingling when inserting it into the belly chakra. Spend a few minutes with your attention focused into the lower abdomen area, palms resting against it. Repeat the exercise two or three times per day.

General information: A well-balanced navel chakra makes you a very pleasant social person. Not only would you emanate desire, joy, happiness, but you will also be sexy. People will be attracted to you. This chakra gives motility, energy, motivation. When the navel chakra is over-energized, you will certainly become lusty, you can lose grip of social conventions, you might become selfish and mean. On the contrary, if your sacral chakra is under-energized, you will lose the wish to be social, your sex appetite can diminish dramatically and you expose your lower abdomen organs to dis-eases.

Solar Plexus Chakra

Position: two inches below the sternum (push with your fingertip – the place where it hurts is the center of the chakra)
Element: fire
Sentence: I can
Color: yellow
Subtle body: mental
Organs: stomach, pancreas, liver, spleen, gallbladder
Issues: ulcer, pancreatitis, diabetes, hepatitis, cirrhosis, colon diseases, biliary dyskinesia, fat deposit on the abdomen, arthritis; low self-esteem, indecision, sensitivity to criticism
When activated: the whole metabolism works properly and hence the entire body (that is properly fed); internal energy, decisiveness, diligence, joy of having things done well, leadership qualities
Exercise: stand up, feet shoulders wide. Point your palms towards the ground, then turn them slowly upwards, as if digging the earthly energy beneath your soles. Don't bend, do it with the fingers, then with the palms, bending the elbows. Pull the energy slowly up along your feet, legs, knees, thighs, root chakra, navel chakra. Insert it into the solar plexus chakra. Do the movement seven times. Feel the tingling in your palms when you grasp the energy, feel the tingling when inserting it into the upper abdomen chakra.

Spend a few minutes with your attention focused into the solar plexus area, palms resting against it. Repeat the exercise two or three times per day.

General information: The balanced plexus chakra will make you a very active person, who enjoys doing his job, and who also proves leadership qualities. The lumbar chakra will make you manifest decision and ease in difficult moments. On the other hand, your body will take full benefit of the food you eat, regulating energy intake from your meals (this is the fire chakra).

Heart Chakra

Position: center of the chest
Element: air
Sentence: I love
Color: green
Subtle body: astral
Organs: heart, lungs, circulatory system, respiratory system, thymus
Issues: lung, shoulder and heart problems; low energy feelings like hatred, envy, fear, jealousy
When activated: it gives a deep and constant feeling of understanding, forgiving and loving the others
Exercise: Stretch your hands over your head, palms facing each other. Feel as if a light ball shines between your hands. In a slow motion, take the ball gently and pull it down, into the

crown chakra. Insert it there. With the palms stretched (fingers together) push the light down your face, along the front of your neck, and into your heart. Do the movement seven times. Feel the tingling in your palms when you grasp the ball, feel the tingling when inserting it into the crown chakra and also when you insert the energy into your heart, palms resting against it. Spend a few minutes with your attention focused into the heart. Then, position your thumbs on the heart and your other fingers on the solar plexus. Pull all fingers together half way, as if uniting the two chakras. Repeat the exercise two or three times per day.

General information: Opening the heart chakra is the first level of linking yourself to the Higher Self. Certainly, this is one of the most important levels, since love is God's frequency. A well-balanced heart chakra gives you feelings of deep peace, compassion and care for others. It also makes you let go of any pain, misery, worry, despair. It brings a kind, gentle smile on your face. People would search for your company, they would tell you their secrets, they would ask for your soothing presence.

Throat Chakra

Position: at the base of your throat, inside between the clavicles
Element: ether
Sentence: I speak
Color: clear blue
Subtle body: causal
Organs: thyroid gland, larynx, esophagus, vocal cords, lower jaw
Issues: hyper/hypo thyroid function, frequent laryngitis or pharyngitis (sore throat)
When activated: lets you fully express not only your feelings, but also your messages in a clear, concise and precise way, letting no doubt about what you want to express. Messages from beyond the known world will be more accessible
Exercise: Stretch your hands over your head, palms facing each other. Feel as if a light ball shines between your hands. In a slow motion, take the ball gently and pull it down, into the crown chakra. Insert it there. With the palms stretched (fingers together) push the light down your face, and into your neck. Do the movement seven times. Feel the tingling in your palms when you grasp the ball, feel the tingling when inserting it into the crown chakra and also when you insert the energy into your neck. Spend a few minutes with your attention focused into the neck, palms resting against it.

General information: when blocked, the neck chakra doesn't allow you to express yourself. You are timid, shy, silent, solitary. When speaking in public places, you choke and despair. At a physical level, you'll suffer from neck diseases and thyroid malfunctions.

Eyebrow Chakra (The Third Eye)

Position: right between the eyebrows, slightly up
Element: light
Sentence: I see
Color: indigo
Subtle body: celestial
Organs: face, nose, eyes, sinus, cerebellum, pituitary gland
Issues: acne, sinusitis, migraines, slow thinking, lack of concentration and clarity, wandering thoughts, not being inspired
When activated: it opens the whole mind to new ideas, it rejuvenates the way you think, lets you intuitively know others. When over-activated, it might bring auditory or visual hallucinations, with symptoms of schizophrenia or paranoia.
Exercise: Stretch your hands over your head, palms facing each other. Feel as if a light ball shines between your hands. In a slow motion, take the ball gently and pull it down, into the crown chakra. Insert it there. With the palms stretched (fingers together) push the light down to your forehead, and into it. Do the movement

seven times. Feel the tingling in your palms when you grasp the ball, feel the tingling when inserting it into the crown chakra and also when you insert the energy in between your eyebrows. Spend a few minutes with your attention focused into the forehead, palms resting against it.

General information: with an unbalanced eyebrow chakra, your mind is rather slow. Ideas don't come when you need them (perhaps only when it's too late), you can't find solutions to your problems, you are ineffective. A balanced third eye chakra will connect you to the Universal mind, the place where all that ever was, is, or will be, is. You will be inspired, prompt with solutions, your mind finds a new meaning to the world. You will cope with the others much better, because your "instincts" work far better.

Crown Chakra

Position: the fontanel (the last portion of the skull that solidified when several months old)
Element: thought
Sentence: I know
Color: violet or white
Subtle body: karmic
Organs: brain, cerebellum, skull, pineal gland
Issues: headaches, brain tumors, poor blood flow, hair loss, poor health, permanent bad

moods, a sense of not belonging to this world – alienation, loneliness

When activated: general good health (if the other chakras are also activated), higher understanding of your being and personal purpose, wisdom, clarity, superiority

Exercise: Stretch your hands over your head, palms facing each other. Feel as if a light ball shines between your hands. In a slow motion, take the ball gently and pull it down, into the crown chakra. Insert it there. Do the movement seven times. Feel the tingling in your palms when you grasp the ball, feel the tingling when inserting it into the crown chakra. Spend a few minutes with your attention focused on the top of your head, palms resting against it.

General information: If the other chakras are somehow connected to the physical body, the crown chakra is the gateway for the Universal energy, and also the gateway to All That Is – to God. This might seem a mere occult mumbo-jumbo, but you'll feel the intensity of the Light when inserting it into the head, during the exercise. You will also feel, after a few days, the intensity of the peace engulfing your person. When well balanced, this chakra gives the sentiment of being perfectly anchored in this realm, it lets the supreme being permanently flow on you. It can make you happy. When over activated, it simply cuts you off from this reality

– you become One with Everything.

Final exercise: on the patterns above, stretch arms and push Reiki along your whole body, down the legs and into the earth. Then bring the earth energy up the body and above your head. Repeat seven times, very slowly, paying attention to the flow of the Reiki.

How You Can Check Your Chakras

First of all, have the chakras chapter listed available to you for reference. Have a blank sheet of paper and a pen and see what is good or wrong with your body or in your life, according to the (very short) chakra description.

For example, take the Root chakra. Before doing this, relax with several slow deep breaths, placing your attention to the process: air intake through the nose, air flow through the larynx, pharynx, trachea, your lungs filling with oxygen. Concentrate then do what you're doing – analyzing your chakra activity.

Position. Point your awareness to the base chakra. If you can't direct the attention on that spot, put your index finger tip on it. Can you feel any sensation at all in that place? Describe them.
Sentence: Think of your life. Are you a strong, dynamic, living being?
Organs: Are all the organs governed by this

chakra all right? Is there any sign of an imbalanced functioning?
Issues: Do you suffer from any disease? Are you poor, struggling, alone?

Take all chakras one by one and allow yourself a serious insight of **who**, **what** and **how** you are. This analysis moment could be crucial for your life: when you know what is wrong, you can fix it easier.

Aura – The Subtle Sign of Your (Im)Perfection

As we showed before, chakras are colored. Some would think this as a strange or forced coincidence: from down to top, from root to crown, chakra colors mimic the rainbow colors.

Light is a pulsing, vibrant physical reality. Some three decades ago, scientist wondered if it is a particle or a wave. Physicists say light is just the visible part of the electromagnetic spectrum, and they say that quarks, positrons, protons, electrons emit light. Could light be an elementary component of matter, or **the** elementary component of matter – as all the adepts of spiritualism sustain?!

Energetic imbalances modify the form of your general aura. A Reiki Master is able to feel the ruptures with his hands, or even see it.

You, too, can see auras with some practice. The steps below are meant to give you just a hint about clear vision. The technique is based on the complementary colors and the afterimage phenomenon, shortly explained as the color you see with eyes closed, after having stared at a brightly colored object: blue after orange, violet after yellow, green after red (and vice versa). Do not think this is just a complementary color trick – with time and practice, you will see **real** aura.

5 Steps to Seeing Auras

1ˢᵗ Step

- Hang a **vividly** colored (**one single color**) object on a white wall. Sit in front of it, at 5-7 feet. Have a good light come from **behind** you (daylight or a 100 W bulb is enough). Have a few deep breaths, to relax. Stare at the object – but not directly – one inch from its margin and past it (I mean, don't focus your look on the wall; just let the look **rest** near the object, because auras are to be seen with the peripheral vision). You may blink, but you are not allowed to change the focus.
- After a 30 second to two minute period, you will notice a thin strip of outlining color coming from the object; its hue is the complementary color of the object on

the wall. Try to observe how wide the color strip could become. **Do not** change focus!
- Rehearse every day. Do the exercise as many times as necessary, until the strip is steady and appears at a first glance.
- Then change the object and repeat with another color.

2nd Step
- Repeat the exercise with a tree. Look past it from a reasonable distance, as to see it entirely. Have the tree projected against the sky, with the sunlight coming from behind. Do it either in the morning, or in the evening, when the light is not too bright.
- After several sessions, you will notice a strip of quivering grayish light bordering the contour of the tree.

3rd Step
- Pick an animal (a cat for example, they would stay still for longer periods) and rehearse.

4th Step
- Put your hand against the white wall.
- By now, you should be able to see its aura in a few seconds. If not, repeat the steps

from the 1st phase until you get results.

5*th* Step

- Have a relative or a friend play the "still object."
- Now, see their aura.

Is Aura Seeing Important?

Not for everybody: if you have never seen an aura, you can't have the huge sentiment of joy at the sight of this wonderfully colored world – it is beyond your understanding.

Also, aura seeing is of no use if you can't figure out a meaning and a purpose to it.

But what if a perfect liar tells you something and you could identify the color of her/his lies? What if you could immediately see when a dog has the intention to bite you, or that a human wants to rob you? What if you could tell when someone close is getting ill before the illness is already installed?

Chapter III – Initiation in Reiki

Can Everyone Become a Reiki Practitioner or a Reiki Master?

Initiating processes and ceremonies occur in practically each and every area of human life: education, administration, religion, etc. Knowledge and a power are handed to the initiated. The power to teach, the power to rule, the power to spread the Light… So anyone can be given the Power, on condition to learn and to practice.

As a matter of fact, at the beginning, Reiki was an initiation practice into esoteric dimensions. In ordinary English, adepts were first introduced to the "theory" of the Universal Energy. After a time, they were "attuned" to that energy, in a mystical ceremony. They had then a practice period, of learning step-by-step how to deal with the Reiki, they were attuned to ever superior levels and finally, after having reached the permanent connection to the Energy, they were given the Master attunement (they had reached sufficient knowledge to be able to attune, to teach Reiki).

Strange as it might be, there is no practical difference between Reiki and any other religious or mystical disciplines on the face of the earth. In the end, priests, gurus, shamans, illuminati, druids, wizards, they all receive knowledge and Powers from their Masters.

Then they can comfort, they can heal, they can absolve, they can energize water, they can protect from evil energies, they can exorcize, etc.

Can then everyone become a Reiki practitioner or a Reiki master? Yes, definitely yes. Reiki is in all of us, as the essential energy that gives us life. But further "performance" is different from case to case.

What Must You Do to Become a Reiki Practitioner?

Mainly, you have to have the attunements and the instruction given by the Master.

The Reiki initiation is a ritual during which the novice is "plugged" to the Universal energy source. It has three components:
- physical – the ritual itself;
- energetic – energetic meridians and centers are "cleaned";
- spiritual – the novice receives, from the Master, a number of Light guides, an amount of Self knowledge and a number of gifts from the Divinity, in order to allow the Self evolve and accomplish its mission in this world.

The whole process requires devotion, practice and belief. Or, belief, practice and devotion – in this order.

Truth is, not everybody reaches the Master level. They don't know what they lose... Once upon a time, they will discover how badly they need the Reiki.

I must confess I was not always a good Reiki student. My first Master attuned me for the first level and then we didn't see each other – because of the distance separating us – for more than two months. In this period, I was supposed to have second and third level attunements, but we couldn't do it.

I was – like blind people – trying my way with a white cane, I was hitting walls, getting back and start it all over again, from the starting point. I was bubbling with vanity, thinking that I can reach the stars all by myself, with the 25-30 books I had read about Reiki.

In reality, I was vain, emptied of elementary modesty and humility. I had no love inside, no love outside. I was missing what is essential in such a stage: guidance, advice, superior knowledge, the warmth of a Master's Reiki. A bit confused by the numerous readings about Reiki, I did not even know what direction to apply to the first symbol, Cho Ku Rei: was it clockwise or anticlockwise?!

I was battering myself for my clumsiness, for my impotence. A strong feeling grew within myself day after day: life was not possible anymore without Reiki (the Force was pushing me forward, despite my clumsiness; I was ripe and ready to be harvested). I had taken a decision.

The day I received my salary, I called a local Master and made an attunement appointment. She agreed after a few questions. Two days later, I was sitting on a stool and having all three initiating levels at once! The Master didn't explain me why she was taking a shortcut. Later that night, I understood: Reiki was already in me since the previous first degree attunement; more than that, my blind efforts, my sincerity and my belief in Reiki did pay, and I was on the good path.

I won't tell you the intimate sensations I lived the next weeks with – until seeing Purgatory, it is hard to see the Heaven.

Important item for this: extraordinary events were unfolding in my life. In two weeks of daily self-treatment, an avalanche of happy coincidences were pouring on top of my life. I was meeting the people I needed, new ideas popped out of my mind... In short, the Universal energy was here, in my chest, pulling things in as if I were a huge magnet for Luck. I was blessed, bliss-ed, I was like Prometheus stealing fire. But not aware of the Action-Reaction Law.

Things are going ever better in my life. I don't need more than it is given to me. Because, in fact, all that I need is given. This book is nothing else than my tribute to Reiki and to humanity. It doesn't matter if this contribution is large or small: I am offering my thanksgiving.

The lesson I am trying to teach you is: **do it**. And pay very close attention to what is to come. Search for a Reiki Master in your vicinity. Google her/him and see for references. Have yourself attuned!

How Much Would an Attunement Cost?

An attunement is priceless. Reiki tradition says the sum is up to the "apprentice." Before thinking of paying, do evaluate: the luxury displayed in the office; possible references; clothing modesty and simplicity; the things you are expecting from Reiki. Browse several websites, for comparison.

Can I Self-Attune Myself to Reiki?

Indeed, you can. It will cost you years of trials, countless failures, painful delays, self-hatred, disappointments, lost opportunities, etc.

A friend of mine is a diplomat mechanical engineer. Hs tried to fix his water taps in the bathroom by himself. He started from the premise of his excellent educational background and the working experience on a construction site. He ended with all the nuts and bolts of his taps strung on the bath floor, not knowing how to put them back. After two days of fights with his wife, he crashed down. His wife called for a plumber who had it all fixed in two hours – out of which one hour and a half were spent in a Homeric laughter. Wasn't my friend a fool?

Why should you do it by yourself? Why waste such an amount of energy and so much time? Why not call for a specialist? How much do you think it will cost you?

Can Reiki Attunements be Done Online?

This is a tricky question. In theory, they can. In practice, they sometimes succeed.

Suppose there is a parking lot filled with 200 cars of different brands. You start them all, and let an automated mobile test bench go to each of them: RPM, emissions, consumption, electrical, headlights alignment, brake power – you name it, I'm not a specialist. Besides the individual results, the test bench does an overall diagnostic, for all the cars in the parking lot.

How many identical diagnoses could you get? 50? 100? 150? Could you tell which car has what malfunction? I don't think so: every car has is own "technical signature." So do we, as humans. Perhaps 1,000,000 times more factors are involved. Then, how could a Master attune many persons s/he wouldn't know?

You could smile at me "Well, you said Reiki is an intelligent energy! That intention is all that matters!"

Rule: This is true. Still, which "car" needs "what" repair?

Can Reiki Attunements be Done in Groups?

First, refer to the rule two lines above.
Second, in a group, the Master has under her/his eyes, s/he could see any slight difference among the "attunes," and ask the Light to come upon each of them (this is a dedicated formula) "upon their merits, possibilities and needs."
What **does that** mean?

Merits: good things you did during this life.
Possibilities: general evolutional stage. i.e. karma, past lives etc. Some may get into a higher state evolution, some must burn their karma.
Needs: some spirits land here to learn/teach lessons and Reiki would help them fulfill their mission.

Above these all, there is an immense "technical" problem: during the attunement, all of your chakras are fully opened to Reiki. Meanwhile, they are fully opened to all energies in the Universe. It is like being exposed nude in a weather lab: snow, blizzard, heat, draught, moist, fog etc. Each of the elements will whip your skin.

One of my previous wives is a strongly bad person; I am being mild: in fact, she is a **demonic** woman. Even now, 16 years from our separation, after being so "strengthened" by Reiki, she is still devastating my energetic layers. Last time she unexpectedly visited me, I needed one full hour to "broom" the house off her tension. Physiologically, symptoms are: tachycardia, high blood pressure, and slight vertigo. Psychologically, I felt: unrest (**before** she showed up!), irritation, lack of concentration, lack of logic, nervousness, finally rage. And, I consider myself a very balanced person!

Energetic vampires are all over the place. They feed with negative emotions: fear, shyness, pride, prejudice, violence, selfishness, egocentrism, hatred, despise, curses, superiority and so on.

Imagine you could have such a person sit next to you, in a group attunement. Imagine how well devils can dissimulate – they could even show bright golden auras. Imagine that, during the attunement, your energy is literally sucked into this black hole... How strong can the

Master be to fight such a beast? How many angels would s/he be needing, while still watching the other attunees?

Take my advice: Go to the attunement by yourself. Pay a dime more, but don't let others to interfere with your nude chakras.

What You Will Learn at Reiki Level 1, 2 and 3

Different Masters have their own different ways to teach Reiki. There are generally two teaching tendencies: having each level separately, and having the first three levels attunement into one single session.

Reiki is **so** flexible that both variants work. I myself think – for practical reasons – that the first variant would work better: the novice's energetic channels and the chakras are opened. Then the student is given the 21 days for self-treatment. I would then teach and attune the 2nd and 3rd level in a single session. The practitioner will then be fully operational and able to discover Reiki under guidance. If weekly guidance sessions are not possible, I'd recommend a manual with all needed procedures and instructions. This self-learning is more complicated though, and leaves the new practitioner at the "mercy" of his/her own logic, diligence, and analysis – with no possibility for either correction or advice.

This is why I strongly recommend a permanent dialog with the Master.

1st level

The student is attuned, as I previously said, for the goal of opening her/his energetic channels and the chakras. S/he is given the hand positions for self-treatment (we'll discus this in detail later). Then, for 21 days, s/he has to work on her/himself with patience and diligence. This period is extremely critical because, after the attunement, the novice's energetic system is not only unbalanced, but also very open to exterior energetic influences. The Reiki (i.e. the intelligent Universal energy) will know how to balance the system, all by itself.

If the initial self-treatment is not done correctly, negative energies from the environment could stick to the novice's body and harm her/him. It should be told here that we live in a permanent energetic connection with the whole humanity, but people around us influence us the most.

I would compare this with the electrical fields coming from indoor and outdoor wiring. At any time, we are like the coil surrounding the magnet in a loudspeaker: the electromagnetic induction makes us enter in resonance with the power source (wiring), at the same frequency. The stronger the current is going through the surrounding wiring, the stronger is the induced electromagnetic field, and the more similar currents our "coil" is producing. The result would be like an imperceptible humming in our mind (like the phenomenon of induction in the loud speaker). Imagine how it is to be living under a high voltage grid: the physical vibration (the humming) turns to shakes, strong shake that would eventually destroy the walls of your body's building.

So, an appropriate self-treatment would pull your core – the magnet – out of the coil, thus protecting you against exterior influences.

A series of bizarre sensations accompany the attunement. Again, this is a function of your personal sensitivity. You might feel tingling either on the skin or inside, heat or cold, pressures, relief, etc. Some could burst into tears or feel like something was torn out of themselves. Sensations vary on a large scale, and there is nothing to worry about. Just tell your Master about your reactions and s/he will explain the **whats** and the **whys**.

Your path to knowledge becomes **very** interesting beginning in the first night and the 21 days and nights to follow. Do your self-treatment with calm and don't give up if strange things happen. The weird phenomena will diminish and finally stop towards the end of the self-treatment. Again, nothing to worry about. Analyze your each sensation, accept it as a gift from Above and give it its correct significance: energies are changing within you, since the Supreme Grid is coming closer and the Energy induction becomes stronger and stronger.

I personally didn't feel anything during the 1st level attunement. It happened in the afternoon and, when I did the first hands treatment, it was like strange currents were crisscrossing my entire body.

2nd and 3rd levels

As I have already stated, I'd rather do these two attunements in a single session. In classical Reiki practice, the novice would given the 2nd level attunement and symbols. Then, after another 21 day period, would be attuned to the 3rd Practitioner level.

Rapid changes happen after this two-level attunement. The Reiki is already stable in your body, the channels are open to the Light. The Master does the needed corrections and then hands the student the keys to Reiki – the symbols.

Spiritual guides. Together with the first level attunement, you will receive a spiritual guide. It is "someone" from the upper dimensions to whom your are assigned for help. The guide will assist you at any time and in whatever would happen in your life. Learn to feel the guide; ask the guide to teach you how to feel it. Have perfect trust in it.

What, in Fact, are Reiki Symbols?

The symbols are mere keys to the Energy. Their existence started in ancient times, when writing was first invented, as graphic representation of gods, but carrying the respective god's energy. It is like each symbol would be a distinct celestial entity. No matter how they evolved, in which part of the world they were created, these "electronic card keys" don't mean anything in themselves. This might seem a very un-orthodox point of view, and please let me explain.

You have this hotel card-key with the number of the room inscribed (the graphic symbol). Can you do anything with it? No, you can't. The important things are within the door you want to open: the card reader, the wiring, the electronic opening device. You place the card into the slot – then the Power and the devices do what they were designed to do: they open the door for you. Another element to be revealed: everything is in place now, the system is working for you, the door in **unlocked**, but you have to **push** it open. The pushing is done through a strong intention.

That is, only your personal drive, your personal effort, are the real door-openers.

The Reiki Symbols Explained

I won't give scholarly definitions or translations. Instead, I give you their real meaning, and paraphrase that meaning for better understanding and practice. You have to know that this is my way of understanding and practicing Reiki; your way might be slightly or very different. Besides a short explanation, I will also give you some of the uses of each symbol.

You can't draw symbols on another person without her/his acceptance – or else you are breaking the person's freewill and you'll pay for it! The only place you are allowed to do it is the Crown chakra, which belongs to the Divinity – if you do it with good intentions, the Divinity might allow His help.

Cho Ku Rei (CKR)

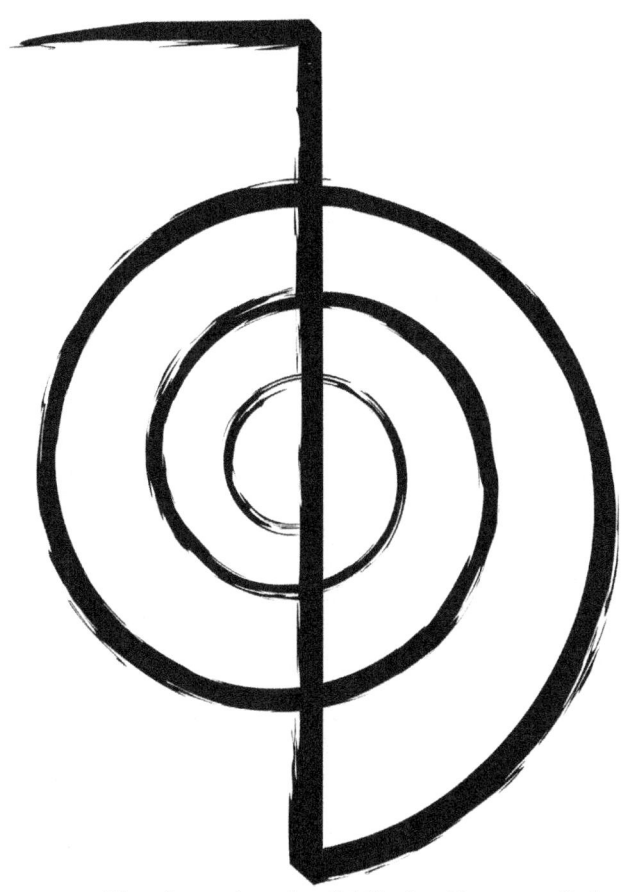

The intention is, "All the Power of the Universe is right here, right now, in my hands!" It is also named the Power Symbol.

This symbol is the channel-opener from the outside in, because it concentrates and amplifies the Reiki flow on the place it is drawn. Uses:

- it has to be drawn in both palms before treatments;
- together with Sei He Ki (the next symbol), it cleans spaces from negative energies;
- together with Sei He Ki, it opens, cleans and protect chakras;
- drawn on food, liquids, crystals, jewels, it cleans and energizes;
- it protects your car when drawn on all sides, top included;
- it protects your personal objects, when drawn upon;
- it can protect from energy stealing, when drawn vice versa on the attacker.

N.B. Discussions have been made if CKR should be used clockwise or anti-clockwise. The direction is not **that** important. The important thing is that **you** chose it, you stick to it and when done the reverse way, your intention will clearly be reversed.

Sei He Ki (SHK)

The translation would be, "Humanity and Divinity unite to be One," or rather "God and I are One," but the intention is, "I am a part of the Divinity like a drop of water is an indefinite part of the ocean, then I am Ocean/Divinity myself." It is also known as the mental and emotional healing key, the symbol of harmony.

Uses:
- draw it when you are depressed, sad, anxious, angry, jealous etc.;
- it opens the chakras and the field from inside out and lets negative energies to be

eliminated from the level it is drawn on;
- a "mirrored" SHK drawn with both hands simultaneously on the crown chakra equalizes the brain hemispheres;
- it helps harmonizing two persons. If you are trying to get yourself harmonized with someone, beware of the other person's negative energy, as you could take a part of it!

Hon Sha Ze Sho Nen (HSZSN)

The translation would be, "The Buddha (the Divinity) in me contacts the Buddha in you"

or, "There is no past, present or future." My intention is, "Since I am Divinity myself, I have no dimension: my here and now is anywhere and anytime!"

HSZSN is the symbol that allows the annihilation of both time and distance. The practitioner can send the Reiki at any point in "space" or "time."

Uses:
- send Reiki to a distant person, using her/his photo or object. You can even send it to a simple name (to a "Mary from Seattle," for example; the intelligence of the Reiki will find Mary);
- send positive energy in the future, to help you on a project;
- send positive energy in the past, to help or to heal (as seen above).

Dai Ko Mio (DKM)

This is the 3rd level symbol. When the practitioner is attuned for DKM, s/he is in fact given the Master level.

An approximate translation would be, "Great place of the shining light," but my intention when using it is, "All that I wish is already within the Divinity so within myself. I open myself to let it materialize. The whole Universe is working with me."

DKM has the highest vibration of all symbols. Its vibration is approximately equal to that of the Cross. DKM connects directly to the Source (at levels 1 and 2 the connection was through the Master). DKM can also be used in combination with all or every other symbol.

A Master would activate her/his healing hands by drawing DKM first, the all the other symbols, and then DKM again. Or, because both are power symbols, just DKM and CKR.

How is a Reiki Attunement Performed?

This is not relevant until you are a Master and you need to attune someone else.

Is it Possible to Learn Reiki in 4 to 5 Days?

As stated before, not quite. Perhaps it is better said that it is not recommendable. But, if there is a strong reason to hurry, or the Master cannot be seen each week, you can have all three level attunements in two days. In extreme cases, in one day.

After that, you are on your own while practicing.

Visualizing Symbol Energy

This exercise is indeed useful, because it sets you personal relationship with each symbol. It also helps you feel the symbol and you will sense its energy awakening while drawing it: in a matter of 3 to 5 seconds, the Reiki will hum in your palms.

How to Visualize Symbol Energy

Stand, feet a shoulder width apart, in a quiet room. Draw the Symbol you wish to sense in both your palms. Clap your hands three times, uttering the symbol's name in loud voice. Light it up (turn it on). Raise it slowly above the crown, as high as you can, put it there as if "in place," let the awareness with it there and let your hands relax beside the body.

Imagine that the symbol is showering fine drops of colored energy allover your body. Stay there for five minutes, until the sensation feels concrete and permanent (if not so, repeat for several days, several times per day). What color does the symbol shine? How intense is the color? How do you feel under the shower? Does anything link you to the color?

Chapter IV – Reiki Uses and Techniques

Hand Positions in Reiki Healing

Before any Reiki (self) treatment, please say the Reiki principles Mikao Usui left us; keep your hands together in front of your heart:
"The secret art of inviting happiness,
The miraculous medicine for all diseases.
At least for today:
>Do not be angry,
>Do not worry,
>Be grateful,
>Work with diligence,
>Be kind to people.

Every morning and evening, join your hands in meditation and pray with your heart.
State in your mind and chant with your mouth.
For improvement of mind and body."

Self Treatment Hand Positions

Draw the symbols in each palm, clap the hands three times, telling the symbol name at each clap.

Each position must be held from three to five minutes. Which hand is where – it doesn't matter, as intention only matters. Keep the fingers close during treatment; otherwise, the energy could be spread and wasted. In each palm center, there is a secondary chakra energized by the symbols; superpose the palm chakra to the center of the treated chakra.

N.B. If impossible because articulation stiffness, body positions can be done with both hands on the front and then with both hands on the back of the body, in a position as correspondent as possible for each chakra. This procedure will lengthen the time allocated to self-treatment, but is more beneficial because the palms cover all internal organs.

1. Head
   - Crown: the two palms laid on top of the head, one beside the other, fingers close.
   - Brow: one hand on the forehead, the other at the base of the skull, at the root of the spine.
   - Eyes: palms facing the eyes, fingers on the forehead. Don't squeeze your patient's nose.
   - Temples: palms on the temples, middle fingers touching on the crown.
   - Ears: palms on the ears, middle fingers touching at the back of the skull.
   - Throat: one hand in front, the other on the

cervical vertebrae, or each hand on one side of the neck. Don't strangle yourself or the patient.

2. Body
- Heart: one hand on the heart (in the middle of the chest), the other on the corresponding position on the back, coming from below. Or the back hand coming from above and covering as much as possible of the thoracic vertebrae.
- Solar plexus: one hand on the plexus, the other on the lower part of the rib cage.
- Navel: one hand below the navel, the other on the kidneys.
- Root: one hand under the scrotum/vagina, the other under the anus.

3. Legs and feet (only when sitting, because the spine must be upright at any time)
- Knees: one hand in front, the other in the back.
- Ankles: either front/back, or laterally.
- Feet: one hand above, the other below.

Quick Self-Treatment

It can be done when in a time crisis. Hold every position for five minutes; lay hands simultaneously:
- one hand on the crown (7th chakra), the other on the root (1st chakra);

- 2nd and 6th chakras;
- 3rd and 5th;
- both hands on the heart chakra.

Healing Others

Put your hands exactly the same locations, except of the fact that some of the positions are done over someone else's body – then hands would be laid differently.

Don't try to heal others before being **attuned** and **trained for**. Ask the patient about her/his medical condition, because Reiki practitioners **do not** diagnose, they only channel the Energy.

Theoretically, you can start healing after the second level attunement. **Better**, if you start after the Master attunement. But **best**, do it only after you have begun to feel and to understand Reiki; after you are in permanent touch (the flow) with the Divine energy.

My personal opinion is that, before doing anything to others, you should first obtain the best results on yourself.

Replacing Negative Energy, Step-by-Step

Try the following exercise:
Stand in the middle of your room, feet at shoulders width. Ask your guide to assist you,

and ask the Divinity to empower you with Reiki.

Now bend your elbows at 80° and bring the hands in front of you, palms upwards, elbows on the ribs; they will be situated at the second chakra level – the Hara, your energetic center. Stay in the position as long as you need to feel the Reiki flow through the crown, down the spine, into the sacral chakra and into your hands. Feel the energy in the palms, feel it concentrate in the palm chakras.

Draw Dai Ko Mio on a wall and say its name in loud voice for three times; then draw Cho Ku Rei on the same wall and tell the name three times. Draw the signs on every wall. Do the same on the ceiling, and finally on the floor.

Come back to the initial position, then get the hands facing each other, at the same height. In this moment, if you did everything well, you can materially feel the energy ball between the palms. Break it – it will follow your will instantly – into two smaller light balls. Get the hands back in the initial position at sacral height. Can you feel the intense energy? If you close your eyes, can you see the bright shining light in your hands?

At the moment when the light/energy is real for you, slowly lift the hands at heart level, turn them towards the wall, take a deep breath and slowly push the energy to and through and past the wall; push when exhaling with force. In the same time, have in mind the intention, "I now push any negative energy out of this room and into the infinity." Get the hands back in initial position. Do the push three times for each wall.

From the initial position, raise the hands and push the energy to, into, and past the ceiling, for three times. Feel the weight of the energy. You may rotate the hands for ease.

Then have the push movement for the floor, too.

In the end, close your eyes and stand quietly in the initial position. How do your hands feel? How is the atmosphere in the room? Did Reiki flow from above and replace the negative energy?

This exercise will give you a correct dimension of the way you should feel Reiki all the time. I repeat, it's only when you can sense the energy **continuously** at **this** intensity that you can start Reiki healing.

Don't take it literally – Reiki will flow through you all the time at the same intensity, you will notice the strength of the energy only the moment your awareness moves to it.

Reiki Healing Benefits

First of all, words can't express the serenity Reiki could give to any practitioner. It is a state of calm, of understanding, of peace, of perpetual near-happiness…

I used to be a normal, sometimes quick-tempered person, especially when driving or when stupid people contradicted me – because I only speak to communicate, and never say things I am not sure about. Reiki allowed me the revelation that anything would happen to me is for a good reason and it has a meaning I should easily understand.

One morning, after having my 3rd level Reiki attunement, I couldn't find my wallet. I was in the air: no money, no credit cards, no ID, no driver license… I turned the entire house upside down, I went in every place I could possibly go the day before, I went to several police precincts, and nothing. Nothing at all for seven days. I would have to ask for new cards (one week + taxes), new ID (five days + taxes), driver license (five more days + taxes). The seventh day I went to the usual Reiki seminar. The Master told me I should be glad for the loss: together with the Master symbol, I had received a new identity – so why shouldn't all my documents be new?!

She taught me a trick: "Go home," she said, "before sleeping, lie in the bed and concentrate on the wallet. Visualize it before of your eyes. Draw a Cho Ku Rei (the Power symbol), a Sei He Ki (the universal connection symbol) and a Hon Sha Ze Sho Nen (the no distance symbol) on the imaginary wallet. Then let your problem be solved by Reiki.

I swear, I found my wallet first thing in

the morning! And I never got angry ever since, despite the numerous challenges I encountered. I said "challenges" because I don't call them "problems" or "troubles" anymore. They are just signs leading me on the right path.

Sorry for the diversion – but in the end it all was about Reiki benefits!

Reiki relaxes instantly. My word, it is sufficient to point your attention to any chakra to let everything go.

Even if you are not a Reiki practitioner, you can ease many of your dis-eases. Let's suppose a forehead ache: put one hand on the forehead and the other on the back of the skull. Stay still in that position for several minutes and it will go.

Tonsillitis: sit and rest your jaw in your palms, as if thinking, for ten minutes, wishing that Reiki cures you. Repeat five or six times in the same day. **Do not** think Reiki is **Light**: tonsillitis is a microbial infection. What happens if you give light to a flower? It will blossom, and so do microbes. Send your tonsillitis the intention to be healed by Reiki.

You dislocated your ankle, the articulation is swollen. Put your hands around it, imagining the Light coming down the spine and right to the hurting tissue. Keep the hands position for 15 minutes. Repeat several times a day. The ankle will heal much faster.

The list of diseases that could be cured or

helped to cure with Reiki is very comprehensive. Anyone who wishes it strong enough could become a Reiki healer sometimes. But even if you would learn Reiki only for your personal benefit, think of how many good things you could give your family.

Using Reiki Together with Other Healing Methods

Crystal therapy. Buy a crystal. After drawing the symbols in your hands, hold the crystal between your palms, as if in a prayer, at the height of your heart chakra. Tell the crystal how you are receiving Light from above, that the Light is flowing through your spine, elbows, hands. Tell it how strong and pure that energy is. Tell it how the light is accumulating in it, is cleaning it, it purifies it. After ¼ hour, you will have your personal crystal. Whenever you need it, it will amplify your Reiki.

Aroma therapy. Aromatherapy uses essential aromatic oils extracted from plants. These oils can be used in combination with Reiki and directly applied on the patient's skin during healing sessions. Also, they can be used with an aroma lamp. In both cases, Reiki enhances the effect of aromas. In fact, most of the Reiki sessions are done – for the reason that aromas help relaxing and concentrate – either with aromatic candles, or with aroma lamps.

Homeopathic therapy: Reiki enhances the effect of the droplets, and helps detoxification.

Allopathic therapy: Reiki accelerates the effect of drugs, helps diminishing side effects and also accelerate the elimination of the residues.

Surgery: Reiki can diminish microbial development, increases blood stream, enhances body response to trauma and accelerates the healing of the tissue.

Chapter V – Reiki Use for Wealth

It is amazing how many uses can be found for Reiki. More amazing though is experiencing it on your own, living all the subtle experiences it can bring.

Reiki and Karma

As you probably know, Karma is the endow people come with in their human existence. Putting it into mundane terms, it is more like an invoice you have to pay during life. An invoice for home suppliers, like you having to pay for mortgage, electricity, water, taxes, sanitation etc. You surely pay for yourself, but you have to pay for your folks, too. Because we come in certain families to help their members pay their bills, too.

When reaching a higher level in Reiki, when the connection to the Divine is stronger and permanent, instead of struggling to pay the "debts" during all the earthly existence, you will be able to accelerate the payments. Not in the sense that they could fall all together on your head in a very short period of time, but in the sense that the sufferance might be less intense and shorter.

Reiki Projects for Wealth

As a part of the daily meditation or self-treatment in Reiki, the practitioner asks the One to gift her/him with "the blessings I am worth of." In other words, the practitioner is aware of the fact that s/he probably does not know her/his karma, and that probably s/he would not be given all the things s/he needs.

Nevertheless, you should try; you might not be given **exactly** what you ask for, but you will be given **something**. The example below is extremely illustrative.

A friend of mine – a notorious journalist in the local community – had given up his job and did something else for a few months. But he missed the newspaper and the journalist life so bad, and he was so bored, that he tried to get back on the news front line. He struggled for months, but nobody seemed to want him.

One day, he finally appealed to Reiki and wrote a project. He stated (this is the short variant) "I want to be called on the phone by the editor of The X newspaper. I want him to accept me. I want him to offer me a good salary. I want him to be happy for his choice."

In a matter of days, he received a phone call from a newspaper editor. He was offered a general manager position. He was invited to come with a new editorial project. He was offered a good salary. But it was not with The X newspaper, it was The Y. Smaller newspaper, smaller salary. The journalist told me he knew why: the One considered he was not worth more.

The project realization took my friend **only one week**! The Law of Attraction applied with Reiki. Precisely, rapidly, in time.

How to Write a Project to Reach Your Goals

Define your goal, in the most exact terms. Define the period of time you expect it to happen. Make you goal clear, short, precise. Write it down. On the blank back of the paper sheet, draw the Reiki symbols. After drawing each, say its name three times. Then activate your hands and keep the note between your palms, as if in a prayer. Think of your goal in the same terms as on the paper. Better, recite those words continuously while in the praying position. Ask your Divinity for help. Put there the intention with all the power of your heart. Do it for 15 minutes or so. Put the project in a secret place, where nobody could find and touch it. Do the concentration on the project as many times as you can, day by day.

After your project was materialized, for 15 minutes, thank your Divinity, your guardian angel, for the help. Then do a sacrifice, offer Them something very personal and important to you: ask for pardon from someone whom you harmed; make an act of charity; stop or diminish smoking/drinking for a period; spend as much time as possible with your folks; fast for a certain period. Anything you feel suitable and proportional to the gift you received.

Good luck with Reiki. May your Divinity send you as much Light as you need and are worth of!